AF575871

LEADERS
OF THE
CIVIL RIGHTS MOVEMENT

www.mascotbooks.com

Leaders of the Civil Rights Movement: A Brief Introduction

Requests for speaking events, extra book copies or permissions should be addressed to dmoore2253@gmail.com.

For more information, please contact:
Mascot Books, an imprint of Amplify Publishing Group
620 Herndon Parkway, Suite 220
Herndon, VA 20170
info@mascotbooks.com

Library of Congress Control Number: 2022901985

CPSIA Code: PRV0523A

ISBN-13: 978-1-64543-855-7

Printed in the United States

This book is dedicated to the young adults of the world, especially our Black and brown children of the African diaspora.

As you journey to pursue your goals and dreams, and find yourself in need of emotional support, encouragement, and inspiration, my desire is for you to draw upon the inspiring stories of the many men and women who gave their blood, sweat, tears, and lives in an effort to free the enslaved Africans and their descendants and secure civil rights for all.

I can't emphasize it enough—there is inspiration and empowerment in the stories that are to be told about the enslaved Africans and their descendants, and these stories should be told regularly and accurately.

"You can do it. Our ancestors did so much more with a lot less!"

LEADERS
OF THE
CIVIL RIGHTS MOVEMENT

-A BRIEF INTRODUCTION-

By Deidra R. Moore-Janvier, Esq.

"YES WE CAN!"
- President Barack Obama

INTRODUCTION

Why Did I Write this Book?

In 2019, the Library of Congress created a virtual portrait gallery titled "African American Activists of the 20th Century." The collection, which is still available online, includes images of notable African American Activists who made history. These individuals overcame adversity and changed the world, paving the way for others to live better lives.

After reviewing these images, I realized that these images of strong, courageous African American people, were too important "to just look at—I wanted to create a way to more actively engage with the collection, and with the lives of these Activists." I thought to myself, "How can I make this a teachable moment for my son, and for other children?"

Inspired, I decided to compile a brief introduction to the lives of some phenomenal people who contributed to the sacrifices made for civil rights of Black people, and ultimately civil rights for all.

The images put out by the Library of Congress, are matched with biographical and background information, along with notable quotes anchored in the times each person lived.

To the younger generations of now, and those to come, always remember that as you search for your place in this world, my hope is that you bring, on your journey, the history of our ancestors. It is so important to keep the stories of their lived experiences alive in the minds of our youth. Always remember that you have the same innate capabilities found in the historical figures depicted on the coming pages. Why not strive to "dream like Dr. Martin Luther King, Jr.; lead like Harriet Tubman; fight like Malcolm X; think like Marcus Garvey; write like Maya Angelou; build like Madam C.J. Walker; speak like Frederick Douglass; believe like Thurgood Marshall; and challenge like Rosa Parks." Remember, Find your V.I.P. Status—meaning your Voice, Identity, and Purpose—and don't be afraid to use it for the good of yourself and others.

We are all capable of becoming, living, and continuing the legacies of these phenomenal people and their phenomenal stories.

-Deidra R. Moore-Janvier

March 2023

"Virtue knows no color line..."

"I had an instinctive feeling that the people who have little or no school training should have something coming into their homes weekly which dealt with their problems in a simple, helpful way...so I wrote in a plain, common-sense way on the things that concerned our people."

"I am only a mouthpiece through which to tell the story of lynching and I have told it so often that I know it by heart. I do not embellish; it makes its own way."

IDA B. WELLS

July 16, 1862 - March 25, 1931

IDA B. WELLS-BARNETT[1] was an outstanding woman reformer of the late nineteenth and twentieth centuries. As a Black female activist, she was outspoken as to human and civil rights, particularly as they related to Black people. Wells became the most famous Black woman in America, particularly "during a period when women, black or white, were permitted only limited participation in public life (Franklin, 1986)."

Wells-Barnett's "crusade for justice" was born of her difficult life circumstances. Her early life in Holly Springs, Mississippi, until her move to Memphis, Tennessee, in 1883, was characterized by personal sacrifices, tragedy, and hardship.

DID YOU KNOW!

- In 1878, Wells experienced a personal tragedy with the death of both of her parents and one of her siblings—during the yellow fever epidemic of 1878 (Duster, 1970; Giddings, 1984).

"After the death of her parents, she assumed responsibility for her siblings (to prevent their separation), even though concerned friends of the family offered to care for them. At age 16, she hired a housekeeper and took a job teaching school in a nearby rural area, where she worked all week, and returned on weekends to care for her siblings (Duster, 1970)."

- In 1883, Wells accepted another teaching position and took her two sisters to Memphis to live with an aunt.

"On a return trip to Memphis from Woodstock, Tennessee, where she taught, she was evicted from the ladies coach (for white women only) when she refused to move. She believed that if blacks stood up for rights granted in Reconstruction legislation, their rights would be preserved. She took legal action and won in the lower courts, but the era of Reconstruction was over, and the state supreme court reversed the decision of the lower court. Wells was devastated by this decision and lost faith that justice would prevail (Giddings, 1984). This incident launched her active crusade for human rights and justice."

- In 1892, her antilynching campaign was launched after Tom Moss, a friend, and his partners in a joint business venture (a grocery store) were removed from the town's jail and lynched. (The three men had been arrested for wounding three white men trying to drive them out of business.). Wells saw lynching as a direct result of the gains blacks were making in the South and as an attempt to stop their progress. Her attacks against lynching infuriated the whites in Tennessee, and a mob of whites destroyed her press while she was on a speaking tour in Philadelphia in 1892.
- By 1924, Wells-Barnett was well known for her independence and refusal to compromise her principles. When she ran for the presidency of the National Association of Colored Women in 1924, she lost the election to Mary McLeod Bethune, who was as diplomatic as Wells-Barnett was uncompromising (Giddings, 1984.

- More about Wells-Barnett's contributions, style, attitude, beliefs, and views of the world can be found in her autobiography, *Crusade for Justice*, edited by her daughter, Alfreda Wells Duster (1970).

ENDNOTES

1 Peebles-Wilkins, Wilma and E. Aracelis Francis. Two Outstanding Black Women in Social Welfare History: Mary Church Terrell and Ida B. Wells-Barnett. *AFFILIA*, vol. 5 No. 4, Winter 1990 pp. 87-100.

"While most girls run away from home to marry, I ran away to teach."

"I cannot help wondering sometimes what I might have become and might have done if I had lived in a country which had not circumscribed and handicapped me on account of my race, that had allowed me to reach any height I was able to attain."

MARY CHURCH TERRELL

September 23, 1863 - July 24, 1954

MARY CHURCH TERRELL,[1] a native of Memphis, Tennessee, who moved to Washington, DC, to teach, was the daughter of emancipated slaves.

She was one of the few Black women in the United States not only to complete college, but to earn a master's degree, taking "gentlemen's courses" (Latin and Greek) at Oberlin College, and to become proficient in three other languages, namely, French, German, and Italian, while studying abroad for 2 years. Her proficiency in languages equipped her to deliver her address on the American racial problem in both French and German at the 1904 meeting of the International Council of Women, held in Berlin, Germany (Sterling, 1988).

During Jane Addams's presidency of the International Congress of Women (later called the Women's International League for Peace and Freedom) Terrell was a delegate to the meeting in Zurich, Switzerland. One of 30 Americans attending the 1919 conference, she described the plight of black Americans in French, German, and Italian (Franklin, 1986; Peebles-Wilkins, 1987; Sterling, 1988).

Terrell was a leader in the fight for racial integration and justice in the United States. She helped to establish, along with Wells-Barnett and others, the National Association for the Advancement of Colored People (NAACP) in 1910 and participated in a wide range of activities of protest and civil disobedience well into her 80s.

More about Terrell can be found in the Mary Church Terrell Papers, housed at the Moorland-Spingarn Research Center, Howard University, Washington, DC.

ENDNOTES

1 Peebles-Wilkins, Wilma and E. Aracelis Francis. *Two Outstanding Black Women in Social Welfare History: Mary Church Terrell and Ida B. Wells-Barnett. AFFILIA*, vol. 5 No. 4, Winter 1990 pp. 87-100.

"The problem of the twentieth century is the problem of the color line."

"Education is that whole system of human training within and without the school house walls, which molds and develops men."

"The cost of liberty is less than the price of repression."

W.E.B. DU BOIS

February 23, 1868 - August 27, 1963

WILLIAM EDWARD BURGHARDT DU BOIS was an American sociologist, historian, civil rights activist, Pan-Africanist, author, writer, and editor. He was born and raised in Great Barrington, Massachusetts[1].

Relying on money donated by neighbors, Du Bois attended Fisk University, a historically black college in Nashville, Tennessee, from 1885 to 1888.[2] His travel to and residency in the South was Du Bois's first experience with Southern racism, which at the time encompassed Jim Crow laws, bigotry, suppression of black voting, and lynchings.[3] After receiving a bachelor's degree from Fisk University, he attended Harvard College (which did not accept course credits from Fisk) from 1888 to 1890, where he was strongly influenced by his professor William James, prominent in American philosophy.[4] Du Bois paid his way through three years at Harvard with money from summer jobs, an inheritance, scholarships, and loans from friends. In 1890, Harvard awarded Du Bois his second bachelor's degree, cum laude, in History.[5] In 1891, Du Bois received a scholarship to attend the sociology graduate school at Harvard.[6]

Racism was the main target of Du Bois's polemics, and he strongly protested against lynchings, Jim Crow Laws and discrimination in education and employment. His cause included people of color everywhere, particularly

Africans and Asians in colonies. He was a proponent of Pan-Africanism and helped organize several Pan-African Congresses to fight for the independence of African colonies from European powers.

Du Bois made several trips to Europe, Africa and Asia. After World War I, he surveyed the experience of American black soldiers in France and documented widespread prejudice and racism in the United States military.

After returning from Europe, Du Bois completed his graduate studies; in 1895 he was the first African American to earn a Ph.D. from Harvard University.[7] He became a professor of history, sociology and economics at Atlanta University.

In 1909 Du Bois was one of the founders of the National Association for the Advancement of Colored People (NAACP).

DID YOU KNOW

In 1897 Du Bois showed great insight when he wrote a speech titled "Strivings of the Negro People." Who knew that the question posed then would be a question posed today, nearly 123 years later.

"Between me and the other world there is ever an unasked question:… How does it feel to be a problem?...One ever feels his two-ness—an American, a Negro; two souls, two thoughts, two unreconciled strivings; two warring ideals in one dark body, whose dogged strength alone keeps it from being torn asunder...he would not Africanize America, for America has too much to teach the world and Africa. He would not bleach his Negro soul in a flood of white Americanism, for he knows that Negro blood has a message for the world. He simply wishes to make it possible for a man to be both a Negro and an American, without being cursed and spit upon by his fellows, without having the doors of opportunity closed roughly in his face."[8]

ENDNOTES

1 Lewis, David Levering (1993). *W. E. B. Du Bois: Biography of a Race* 1868–1919. New York City: Henry Holt and Co. p. 11. ISBN 9781466841512. [Du Bois] would unfailingly insist upon the 'correct'

pronunciation of his surname. 'The pronunciation of my name is Due Boyss, with the accent on the last syllable,' he would patiently explain to the uninformed."

2 Lewis, Catharine, "Fisk University", in Young, p. 81.

3 Lewis, pp. 56–57.

4 Lewis, pp. 72–78.

5 Lewis, pp. 69–80 (degree); p. 69 (funding); p. 82 (inheritance). Du Bois was the sixth African American to be admitted to Harvard.

6 Lewis, p. 82.

7 Lewis, p. 90.

8 Quoted by Lewis, pp. 143–145.

"You must never be fearful about what you are doing when it is right."

"I would like to be known as a person who is concerned about freedom and equality and justice and prosperity for all people."

"Each person must live their life as a model for others."

JAMES WELDON JOHNSON

June 17, 1871 - June 26, 1938

JAMES WELDON JOHNSON was a man of boundless talent. He had an extraordinary career, spanning from being an American educator, lawyer, author, songwriter, diplomat, and civil rights activist. Johnson was a high school principal by age 21. He spoke at least four languages, Spanish, French, Latin, and of course English. In 1894 he graduated from (Clark) Atlanta University. Upon graduating from (Clark) Atlanta University, Johnson returned to Jacksonville, Florida, where he taught at Stanton, a school for African American students. He was the first Black man admitted to the Florida bar since the Reconstruction Era.

He was also one of the first African American professors at New York University. Later in life he was a professor of creative literature and writing at Fisk University.

Like many of his time, James Weldon Johnson rose up from indentured servitude to exemplify the caliber of talent that was unable to contribute to American society due to the legacy of segregation. He was part of the Black intellectual elite who led the United States to enlightenment after Radical Reconstruction.[1]

- 1899: Johnson's first success as a writer was the poem "Lift Ev'ry Voice and Sing"; the hymn often referred to as the "Black National Anthem."
- 1900: On February 12, "Lift Ev'ry Voice and Sing" was performed for the first time by 500 school children at Stanton (Jacksonville, Florida), in celebration of President Abraham Lincoln's birthday.
- 1901: "Lift Ev'ry Voice and Sing" was set to music by his brother J. Rosamond Johnson.

At the dawning of what would become the modern civil rights movement, he forged a record of accomplishment that defied the odds. The Library of America now presents a collection of his writings that displays the many facets of a complex and impassioned writer.[2]

The Autobiography of an Ex-Colored Man (1912), Johnson's first book, is a novel that on its original anonymous publication was taken by many for an actual memoir. A groundbreaking work of modern fiction, it powerfully describes the inner development of a gifted, socially alienated man as he tries to come to terms with the constraints of racism.[3]

DID YOU KNOW

In *The Essential Writings of James Weldon Johnson,* he offered two important things, "words of caution" and a "personal pledge."

"I offer now some words of caution. We are in constant danger of growing to feel that all the ills we suffer are due to race prejudice, and so, of falling into the habit of framing excuses for our own shortcomings. We must try to avoid that danger. We should squarely face our failings. And, too, we should remember that, if race prejudice were abolished today, there would remain to us tomorrow all the ills that are common to humanity. That, however, is exactly the point we are striving to reach, the point where we can enter the race, not handicapped back of the line, but starting from scratch.

In the situation into which we are thrown, let each one of us, let the whole race, be ceaselessly on guard against the loss of spiritual integrity. So long as we maintain that integrity we cannot be beaten down, not in a thousand years. For instance, we suffer the humiliations of Jim-Crowism; but we are not vitally inured so long as we are Jim-Crowed in soul. If it is necessary for me to travel on the railroad in a Jim-Crow state, I am in all probability forced to climb into a Jim-Crow car; but the injury inflicted on me is only external, unless I should feel within myself that I am in my right place, that I am where I belong. Each time one of us voluntarily and unnecessarily Jim-Crows himself, he is undermining his spiritual integrity. We must often permit mere timidity and break through the barriers whenever we are able to do it. We often take discrimination for granted where there actually is none or where it is so indefinite that a little courage and pressure would sweep it away. Each time we break through or sweep away discrimination we make it easier for the next time and the next one.

This is a struggle in which time after time we are compelled to yield ground; let us never yield ground spiritually."[4]

"The pledge to myself which I have endeavored to keep through the greater part of my life is:

I will not allow one prejudiced person or one million or one hundred million to blight my life. I will not let prejudice or any of its attendant humiliations and injustices bear me down to spiritual defeat. My inner life is mine, and I shall defend and maintain its integrity against all the powers of hell."[5]

ENDNOTES

1 Jaynes, G. D. (2005). Johnson, James Weldon (1871–1938). In *Encyclopedia of African American Society* (Vol. 1, pp. 472-472). SAGE Publications, Inc., https://www.doi.org/10.4135/9781412952507.n35

2 James Weldon Johnson: *Writings: The Autobiography of an Ex- Colored Man;* Along This Way; essays and editorials; selected Poems By: James Weldon Johnson

3 James Weldon Johnson: *Writings: The Autobiography of an Ex- Colored Man*; Along This Way; essays and editorials; selected Poems By: James Weldon Johnson

4 *The Essential Writings of James Weldon Johnson* (Modern Library Classics) by James Weldon Johnson, Rudolph Byrd, (Pages 317-318)

5 *The Essential Writings of James Weldon Johnson* (Modern Library Classics) by James Weldon Johnson, Rudolph Byrd, (Pages 317-318)

"Without faith, nothing is possible.
With it, nothing is impossible."

"The whole world opened to me when I learned to read."

"Invest in the human soul, who knows, it
may be a diamond in the rough."

MARY MCLEOD BETHUNE

July 10, 1875 - May 18, 1955

MARY JANE MCLEOD BETHUNE was an American educator, stateswoman, philanthropist, humanitarian, and civil rights activist. It was at the age of ten that she formally entered school in South Carolina. "As she learned, she shared the knowledge with the community and her family by teaching others to read and helping local farmers calculate their wages. Before she was able to decide what to do with her life, she started with educating others, and ultimately her love for teaching would guide her."[1]

She later attended Seminary and Bible College with the hope of becoming a missionary. She was later disappointed when she was told no, but she was not deterred. She took the disappointment, which could have been a setback, and turned it into determination.[2]

- 1904: In September, with $1.50 in her pocket, and looking to start a school, Bethune made her way to Daytona Beach. On October 3, 1904, she opened the Daytona Literary and Industrial School for the Training of Negro Girls.[3] She rented a small house for $11.00 per month. She made benches and desks from discarded crates, and acquired other items through charity; the students made ink for pens from elderberry juice, and pencils from burned wood.

- 1919: The school had made its third name change, transitioning form Daytona Educational and Industrial Institute to Daytona Normal and Industrial Institute.[4]
- 1923: The all-girls school began the process of merging with Cookman Institute, a coed school led by the Methodist Church.[5] In 1925 the merger was complete, and both schools collaborated to become the Daytona Cookman Collegiate Institute.[6]
- 1931: The school became officially known as Bethune-Cookman College.[7]
- 1935: Mary McLeod, at the age of 60 founded the first national coalition of African American women's organizations (now known as The National Council of Negro Women).

The National Council of Negro Women's mission was to advance the opportunities and the quality of life for African American women, their families, and communities.

DID YOU KNOW

When one of Bethune's students became violently ill, she took her to the nearest hospital. She convinced the staff of Dr. C.C. Bahannin's hospital, to admit the child in spite of their policy to admit Whites only. Having been denied permission to visit her student, Bethune managed to gain entrance to the hospital only to discover that her student had been left on the hospital porch unattended. Her anger compelled her to act. In 1911, she opened the first Black hospital in Daytona Beach on the grounds of her school.[8]

ENDNOTES

1 *Mary McLeod Bethune in Florida: Bringing Social Justice to the Sunshine State*, by Dr. Ashley N. Robertson; p. 12.

2 Id.

3 Id.

4 *Mary McLeod Bethune in Florida: Bringing Social Justice to the Sunshine State*, by Dr. Ashley N. Robertson; p. 18.

5 Id.

6 Id.

7 Id.

8 Id.

"Having standards isn't really for anyone else. You should want to have them for yourself."

"What is your purpose? Why are you here? Start small and find out."

"To struggle and battle and overcome and absolutely defeat every force designed against us—is the only way to achieve."

NANNIE HELEN BURROUGHS

May 2, 1879 - May 20, 1961

NANNIE HELEN BURROUGHS was an African American theologian, educator, philosopher, activist, intellectual, feminist, and businesswoman in the United States. "Burroughs had a big vision for her race and a special responsibility to women and girls. Her life's mission was to create opportunities for black women in spaces where they scantily existed."[1]

At the young age of twenty-one, she gave a speech, at the National Baptist Convention, in Richmond, Virginia, titled: "How the Sisters are Hindered from Helping." Her speech won her fame and recognition. Fueled by her deep religious convictions, she began the fight to gain greater recognition for women in church decision-making.

Because of her unusual visibility at the convention, a man noted "Who's that young girl? Why don't' she sit down? She's always talking. She's just an upstart." Burroughs responded, "I might be an upstart, but I am just starting up."

- 1901: True to her words, she spearheaded the Women's Auxiliary to the Baptist Convention. She served as Secretary for 47 years until she was elected president in 1948.
- 1906: She introduced Women's Day to the Baptist Church. The purpose was to teach women to become public speakers and leaders in the community.
- 1907: Burroughs received an honorary master's degree from Eckstein Norton University, a historically black college in Cane Spring Bullitt County, Kentucky.
- 1909: She founded the National Training School for Women and Girls, Inc., in Washington, DC.
- 1964: The school that Burroughs founded in 1909 as the National Training School for Women and Girls in Washington, DC, was renamed the Nannie Helen Burroughs School in her honor; and began operating as a co-ed elementary school.

DID YOU KNOW

Before becoming the founder of the National Training School for Women and Girls in Washington, DC, which she started in 1909, Burroughs sought a teaching position in Washington, DC. When she did not receive it, she moved to Philadelphia, Pennsylvania, and became associate editor of *The Christian Banner,* a Baptist newspaper. Burroughs returned to Washington, DC. where, despite receiving a high rating on the civil service exam, she was refused a position in the public school system. Burroughs took a series of temporary jobs including office building janitor and bookkeeper for a small manufacturing firm, hoping to eventually become a teacher in Washington, DC. She then accepted a position in Louisville as secretary of the Foreign Mission Board of the National Baptist Convention, where she was employed as an editorial secretary and bookkeeper.

ENDNOTES

1 Burroughs, Nannie Helen, 1879-1961, author. *Nannie Helen Burroughs: A Documentary Portrait of an Early Civil Rights Pioneer, 1900-1959* / edited and annotated by Kelisha B. Graves. Notre Dame, Indiana: University of Notre Dame Press, 2019.

"A people without the knowledge of their past history, origin, and culture is like a tree without roots."

"If you haven't confidence in self, you are twice defeated in the race of life. With confidence, you have won even before you have started."

"The pen is mightier than the sword, but the tongue is mightier than them both put together."

MARCUS GARVEY

August 17, 1887 - June 10, 1940

MARCUS MOSIAH GARVEY, JR. was a Jamaican-born political leader, publisher, journalist, entrepreneur, and gifted speaker. He is a monumental, internationally acclaimed Black philosopher who has influenced the independence movement of every black nation in the world, ranging from the Nation of Islam to the Rastafari movement (which proclaim Garvey as a prophet) and the Black Power Movement of the 1960's. He spent his life working towards African self-awareness, self-reliance, and political and economic liberation. His ideas and beliefs became known as 'Garveyism'. Garveyism intended persons of African ancestry in the diaspora to "redeem" the continent of Africa and put an end to European colonialism. He started a "back to Africa" movement hoping to give African Americans the chance to go back to their motherland of Africa.

- 1901: Up to the age of 14, Garvey attended a local church school; further education was unaffordable for the family. At 14 years old, he became a printer's apprentice.[1]
- 1903: Garvey traveled to Kingston, Jamaica, and soon became involved in union activities.[2]

- 1910: Garvey left Jamaica and began traveling throughout the Central American region. His first stop was Costa Rica, where he lived with an uncle for several months and worked as a time keeper on a banana plantation.[3]
- 1911: Garvey moved to Colón, Panama, and before returning to Jamaica in 1912, he published a small newspaper, called *La Prensa (The Press)*.[4]
- 1912-14: After years of working in the Caribbean, Garvey left Jamaica to live in London, where he attended Birkbeck College, taking classes in law and philosophy.[5]
- 1914: After returning to Jamaica, Garvey, at 27 years old, founded the Universal Negro Improvement Association and African Communities League, commonly abbreviated as (UNIA).[6]

The UNIA was founded to work for the advancement of people of African ancestry around the world. Its motto was "One God! One Aim! One Destiny!" and its slogan was "Africa for the Africans, at home and abroad!"[7]

1916: Garvey moved to the United States and established a UNIA branch in New York City's Harlem district.[8]

DID YOU KNOW

"Marcus Garvey arrived in New York on March 23, 1916. By this time the United States had replaced Panama as the major destination for West Indian emigrants. Some 30,000 persons from Jamaica alone moved permanently to the United States between 1911 and 1921. Most of these went to New York. Most West Indians in New York in those days lived in Harlem, the city's major Black community. By 1920 almost one out of every five Black people in Harlem was a West Indian. Many of today's Black native New Yorker's are in fact the descendants of this generation of West Indian emigrants."[9]

"Harlem was an immigrant community in other ways too. Most of its population consisted of refugees from the racism of the American South. Even its native New York-born population had only moved there recently from other parts of the city."[10]

ENDNOTES

1 Tony Martin, Marcus Garvey, *Hero: A First Biography*, Vo 1. (Dover, Mass.: The Majority Press, 1983), 8-9.

2 Martin, Marcus Garvey, *Hero*, 8-9.

3 Martin, Marcus Garvey, *Hero*, 15.

4 Martin, Marcus Garvey, *Hero*, 16.

5 Martin, Marcus Garvey, *Hero*, 18-19.

6 Martin, Marcus Garvey, *Hero*, 27-28.

7 Martin, Marcus Garvey, *Hero*, 31-32.

8 Martin, Marcus Garvey, *Hero*, 38.

9 Martin, Marcus Garvey, *Hero*, 38.

10 Martin, Marcus Garvey, *Hero*, 38.

"Each of you, as an individual, must pick your own goals. Listen to others, but do not become a blind follower."

"Where you see wrong or inequality or injustice, speak out, because this is your country. This is your democracy. Make it. Protect it. Pass it on."

THURGOOD MARSHALL

July 2, 1908 - January 24, 1993

THURGOOD MARSHALL was an American lawyer who served as Supreme Court Justice from 1967 until 1991, making him the 96th justice and its first African American justice. Prior to his judicial service, Marshall successfully argued several cases before the Supreme Court, winning almost every case he tried. His most famous case as a lawyer was Brown v. Board of Education of Topeka, (1954), the case in which the Supreme Court ruled that "separate but equal" public education, as established by Plessy v. Ferguson, was not applicable to public education because it could never be truly equal. He argued that racial segregation in public education is a violation of the Equal Protection Clause.

- 1933: Thurgood Marshall graduated from the Howard University School of Law. He established a private legal practice in Baltimore.
- 1940: Marshall founded the NAACP Legal Defense and Educational Fund.
- 1961: President John F. Kennedy appointed Marshall to the United States Court of Appeals for the Second Circuit.

- 1965: President Lyndon B. Johnson appointed Marshall as the United States Solicitor General.
- 1967: President Johnson successfully nominated Marshall to succeed retiring Associate Justice Tom C. Clark.

DID YOU KNOW

Marshall was born in Baltimore, Maryland. His original name was Thoroughgood, but he shortened it to Thurgood. His father, William Canfield Marshall, worked as a railroad porter, and his mother Norma Arica (Williams), as a teacher; they instilled in him an appreciation for the United States Constitution and the rule of law. Marshall first learned how to debate from his father, who took Marshall and his brother to watch court cases; they would later debate what they had seen. The family also debated current events after dinner. Marshall said that although his father never told him to become a lawyer, he "turned me into one. He did it by teaching me to argue, by challenging my logic on every point, by making me prove every statement I made."

"There is no future for a people who deny their past."

"Only legislative, judicial, and executive action can completely guarantee the victory of the free world."

"Unless man is committed to the belief that all mankind are his brothers, then he labors in vain and hypocritically in the vineyards of equality."

ADAM CLAYTON POWELL, JR.

November 29, 1908 - April 4, 1972

ADAM CLAYTON POWELL, JR. was a Baptist pastor and an American politician, who represented Harlem, New York City, in the United States House of Representatives (1945–71). He was the first person of African American descent to be elected from New York to Congress. In 1928 Oscar Stanton De Priest of Illinois was the first Black person to be elected to Congress in the 20th century; Powell was the fourth. Re-elected for nearly three decades, Powell became a powerful national politician of the Democratic Party, and served as a national spokesman on civil rights and social issues. He also urged United States presidents to support emerging nations in Africa and Asia as they gained independence after colonialism.

In 1961, after 16 years in the House, Powell became chairman of the Education and Labor Committee, the most powerful position held by an African American in Congress. As Chairman, he supported the passage of important social and civil rights legislation under presidents John F. Kennedy and Lyndon B. Johnson. Following allegations of corruption, in 1967 Powell was excluded from his seat by Democratic Representatives-elect of the 90th Congress, but he was re-elected and regained the seat in the 1969

United States Supreme Court ruling in Powell v. McCormack. He lost his seat in 1970 to Charles Rangel and retired from electoral politics.

DID YOU KNOW

Adam Clayton Powell Jr., family surname was originally "Dunning." In the 1860 census, Powell's paternal grandmother, Salley Dunning is listed as a free mulatto, as were her mother, grandmother, and siblings. Sally never identified the father of Adam Clayton Powell Sr., born in 1865. She appeared to have named her son after her older brother Adam Dunning, listed on the 1860 census as a farmer and the head of their household. In 1867 Sally Dunning married Anthony Bush, a mulatto freedman. All the family members were listed under the surname Dunning in the 1870 census.

The family changed its surname to Powell when they moved to Kanawha County, West Virginia, as part of their new life there. According to Charles V. Hamilton, a 1991 biographer of Powell, Anthony Bush "decided to take the name Powell as a new identity," and this is how they were recorded in the 1880 census.

"You must never be fearful about what you are doing when it is right."

"I would like to be known as a person who is concerned about freedom and equality and justice and prosperity for all people."

"Each person must live their life as a model for others."

ROSA PARKS

February 4, 1913 - October 24, 2005

ROSA PARKS was an American activist during the Civil Rights Movement, best known for her pivotal role in the Montgomery Bus Boycott. The United States Congress called her "the first lady of civil rights" and "the mother of the freedom movement." On December 1, 1955, in Montgomery, Alabama, Parks rejected a bus driver's order to relinquish her seat in the colored section to a white passenger, after the whites only section was filled. Parks' prominence in the community and her willingness to become a controversial figure inspired the black community to boycott Montgomery buses for over a year, the first major direct action campaign of the post-war Civil Rights Movement. Parks' act of defiance and the Montgomery bus boycott became important symbols of the movement. She became an international icon of resistance to racial segregation.

- 1955: On December 4, 1955, plans for the Montgomery Bus Boycott were announced at Black churches in the area. Over 35,000 handbills were printed announcing a bus boycott.
- 1955: On December 5, 1955, Parks was tried on charges of disorderly conduct and violating a local ordinance. The trial lasted thirty minutes. After being found guilty and fined $10, plus $4 in court costs,

Parks appealed her conviction and formally challenged the legality of racial segregation. Her case became bogged down in state courts.

DID YOU KNOW

Parks was not the first person to resist bus segregation, but the National Association for the Advancement of Colored People (NAACP) believed that she was the best candidate for challenging a court case after her arrest for civil disobedience. It was the case of Browder v. Gayle that succeeded. On February 1, 1956, a civil rights attorney named Fred Gray organized and filed a lawsuit in federal court on behalf of Claudette Colvin, Aurelia Browder, Susie McDonald, Jeanetta Reese, and Mary Louise Smith—each of whom were arrested in Montgomery for not giving up their bus seats before Rosa Parks. On June 5, 1956, the United States District Court for the Middle District of Alabama issued a ruling declaring the state of Alabama and Montgomery's laws mandating public bus segregation as unconstitutional. State and local officials appealed the case to the United States Supreme Court. The Supreme Court summarily affirmed the District Court decision on November 13, 1956. One month later, the Supreme Court declined to reconsider, and on December 20, 1956, the court ordered Montgomery and the state of Alabama to end bus segregation permanently—and the Montgomery Bus Boycott was called off.

"I'm sick and tired, of being sick and tired."

"Forget what hurt you, but never forget what it taught you."

"Never to forget where you came from, and always praise the bridges that carried us over."

"If I fall, I'll fall five feet four inches forward in the fight for freedom."

FANNIE LOU HAMER

October 6, 1917 - March 14, 1977

FANNIE LOU HAMER, an African American voting and women's rights activist, community organizer, and a leader in the Civil Rights Movement. She was born in Montgomery County, Mississippi. She grew up in poverty. At 27 years old, she married Perry Hamer, and they both worked on the Mississippi plantation owned by B. D. Marlowe.

"In the summer of 1961, Hamer attended a meeting led by volunteers of the Student Non-Violent Coordinating Committee (SNCC); and the Southern Christian Leadership Conference (SCLC). She learned of the constitutional right to vote, and the efforts of others to deny such right to African Americans. She became a member of SNCC and in 1962 led 17 volunteers to register to vote at the Indianola, Mississippi Courthouse. There she was denied the right to vote due to an unfair literacy test.

After attending a program that teaches one how to pass the literacy test, she and few others headed to the Courthouse to register to vote. When the bus reached approximately 25 miles of the voter registration headquarters—the bus driver stopped at a restaurant, allowing folks to get some food, and to use the restrooms. That effort was immediately thwarted. For no comprehensible reason, Fannie Hamer and others were arrested. The bus driver was fined $100.00 for charges that the bus was too Yellow.

It looked too much like a school bus was the allegation. Mrs. Hamer was taken to jail along with several others, where she was brutally beaten at the direction of and at the hands of the police at the jailhouse. She sustained lifelong injuries, a blood clot in the artery in her left eye; permanent injury to her right kidney; and severe leg injury.

The brutal beatings were some of the things African Americans went through, particularly in the Southern states like Mississippi, when all they attempted to do was exercise their right to vote, while simultaneously, requesting to be treated like a human being.

The Justice Department brought a lawsuit against the five law officials involved in the false arrest and brutalization of Mrs. Hamer and the other four people who were arrested, with her.

The Justice Department, brought forward the waitresses in the restaurant, the bus driver, and the two black men the prison officers forced to beat Mrs. Hamer with the blackjack, before the officers further beat Mrs. Hamer in her head with the blackjack themselves. Each of whom told the Court that Mrs. Hamer and the other four people from the bus, did not do anything wrong—that day they were arrested. However, the officers were not found to have violated any one's civil rights.

After two attempts at taking the literacy test, Mrs. Hamer was successful and became a registered voter in the State of Mississippi."[1]

"In 1964, Mrs. Hamer helped co-founded the Mississippi Freedom Democratic Party. In August of that year, she attended the National Democratic Convention in Atlantic City, New Jersey where she challenged the seating of the regular delegation from Mississippi. They offered Mrs. Hamer 2 votes at large, as a compromise, in the convention, but she did not accept the compromise, stating that after 100 years of having the legal right to vote with the passing of the 15th Amendment in 1865, and with having more than 63,000 registered with the Mississippi Freedom Democratic Party, two votes at large did not mean anything."[2]

"In January, 1965, Mrs. Hamer along with two other candidates from the Freedom Democratic Party went to the door of the House of Representative, (knowing they would not be permitted to enter), to contest the seating of the five representatives of Mississippi—and they were turned away, without being able to even go in to contest their seating. Their concerns being primarily to explain that in a state where 42 percent of the people can't register, that these five representatives were not representing all the people of the state of Mississippi. Mrs. Hamer and the other two candidates were ready to state that it is time that someone be in Congress who truly represent the people of the state of Mississippi.

Apparently on that date, there were 149 Congressmen that stood up against these five people looking to be seated. Mrs. Hamer saw this as some progress. She remained committed to the cause."[3]

"Mrs. Hamer was not interested in the Voting Bill that was passed a week prior, in 1965. She pointed out, "I am not looking for a Voting Rights Bill in 1965, when in 1870, with the passage of the 15th Amendment, we were afforded the same voting rights then as they are offering us now, in 1965. As she correctly pointed out, with the passage of the 15th Amendment, and as part of the agreement to allow Mississippi, as a former confederate state, to re-enter the Union, it must agree to not do anything to disenfranchise the African American voting rights. She rightfully pointed out that there is a violation of the 13th, 14th and 15th Amendments of the Constitution that should be addressed."[4]

In 1971 Mrs. Hamer ran for the Mississippi State Senate.

DID YOU KNOW?

Fannie Lou Hamer is buried in her hometown of Ruleville, Mississippi. Her tombstone is engraved with one of her famous quotes, "I am sick and tired of being sick and tired." Her primary memorial service, held at a church, was completely full. An overview service was held at Ruleville Central High School, with over 1,500 people in attendance. Andrew Young, United States Ambassador to the United Nations, spoke at the Ruleville Central High School service, saying: "None of us would be where we are now had she not been there then!"

ENDNOTES

1 Author: Chana Kai Lee; *For Freedom's Sake: The Life of Fannie Lou Hamer.*

2 Author: Chana Kai Lee; *For Freedom's Sake: The Life of Fannie Lou Hamer.*

3 Author: Chana Kai Lee; *For Freedom's Sake: The Life of Fannie Lou Hamer.*

4 Author: Chana Kai Lee; *For Freedom's Sake: The Life of Fannie Lou Hamer.*

"Courage, after all, is not being unafraid, but doing what needs to be done in spite of fear."

"If we do not save the environment, then whatever we do in civil rights will be of no meaning, because then we will have the equality of extinction."

"Institutional practices, it seems, perpetuate themselves mostly by their invisibility."

"We do what we have to, so we can do what we want to."

JAMES FARMER, JR.

January 12, 1920 - July 9, 1999

JAMES LEONARD FARMER, JR. was an extraordinary American civil rights advocate. He was a leader in the Civil Rights Movement, who pushed for non-violent protests to dismantle segregation. Inconceivably, as it may seem, Farmer began formulating the notion of "dismantling segregation," from the tender age of three."[1]

"According to Farmer, he was out with is mother, Pearl Marion Houston Farmer, in Holly Springs, Mississippi, and they arrived at a Woolworth's. He wanted a Coca Cola to drink so he asked his mother if he could have one. She immediately told him "no," but the toddler persisted. He was apparently argumentatively confident, even at this young age. Despite repeated "nos" to his demands, Farmer pointed out that another child was, indeed getting a Coke from his mother in the store. Farmer apparently thought his mother was unaware that the store provided this luxury. Farmer intoned, "That boy is enjoying a Coke, so why can't I?" He vividly recalls that his mother said sternly, "Because he is white and you are not."[2]

"So began a tectonic shift in Farmer's thinking. It was up to that moment, inconceivable that this son of a professor and preacher who lived in relatively affluent circumstances could not gain a straightforward public purchase of a beverage. It was, however, not possible, and Farmer would spend a lifetime trying to excavate the roots of this "why?"[3]

- 1934: Farmer was a child prodigy; as a freshman in 1934 at the age of 14, he enrolled at Wiley College, a historically black college where his father was teaching in Marshall, Texas.
- 1935: Farmer's debate team beat U.S.C. the national champions, and Farmer was an integral part of such defeat. He debated in front of 2,000 people; and it was his phrase "stop lynchings now!" that garnered him a standing ovation, with a thunderous applause.
- 1941: The life of James Farmer, Jr. was dedicated to a simple and profound purpose revealed when his father asked him what he would do with his collegiate and seminary education upon his graduation from Howard University in 1941 at the age of twenty-one. Farmer replied with two words: "Destroy segregation!"[4]
- 1942: Farmer co-founded the Committee of Racial Equality in Chicago. It was later called the Congress of Racial Equality (CORE), and was dedicated to ending racial segregation in the United States through non-violence.
- 1961: Farmer was the initiator and organizer of the first Freedom Ride, which eventually led to the desegregation of interstate transportation in the United States.
- 1968: Farmer ran for U.S. Congress as a Liberal Party candidate backed by the Republican Party, but lost to Shirley Chisholm.
- 1969: The newly elected Republican President Richard Nixon offered Farmer the position of Assistant Secretary of the Department of Health, Education and Welfare (now Health and Human Services).

DID YOU KNOW

The following quote was chiseled in stone at James L. Farmer, Jr.'s memorial at the University of Mary Washington, in Fredericksburg, Virginia: "Freedom and equality are inherent rights in the United States: therefore, I encourage young people to take on the task by standing up and speaking out on behalf of people denied those rights. We have not yet finished the job of making our country whole."

ENDNOTES

1 James Farmer, Jr.: *The Great Debater.* By Ben Voth (Lanham, MD: Lexington Books, 2017), pp.1-5.

2 Voth, *The Great Debater*, pp-1-5.

3 Voth, *The Great Debater*, pp-1-5.

4 Voth, *The Great Debater*, pp-1-5.

"The emotional, sexual, and psychological stereotyping of females begins when the doctor says: 'It's a girl.'"

"In the end anti-black, anti-female, and all forms of discrimination are equivalent to the same thing: anti-humanism."

SHIRLEY CHISHOLM

November 30, 1924 - January 1, 2005

SHIRLEY CHISHOLM was an American politician, educator, and author. In 1968, she became the first Black woman elected to the United States Congress, and represented New York's 12th congressional district for seven terms from 1969 to 1983. In 1972, she became the first Black candidate for a major party's nomination for President of the United States, and the first woman to run for the Democratic Party's presidential nomination. In 2015, Chisholm was posthumously awarded the Presidential Medal of Freedom.

"The future belongs to those who prepare for it today."

"I'm for truth, no matter who tells it. I'm for justice, no matter who it's for or against."

"If you have no critics you'll likely have no success."

MALCOLM X

May 19, 1925 - February 21, 1965

MALCOLM X was an American Muslim minister and human rights activist. Some saw him as a courageous advocate for the rights of Blacks, a man who indicted white America in the harshest terms for its crimes against Black Americans. Others accused him of preaching racism and violence. He has been called one of the greatest and most influential African Americans in history. He is credited with raising the self-esteem of Black Americans and reconnecting them with their African heritage. He is largely responsible for the spread of Islam in the Black community in the United States. Many African Americans, especially those who lived in cities in the northern and western United States, felt that Malcolm X articulated their complaints concerning inequality better than the mainstream Civil Rights Movement did. In the late 1960s, increasingly radical Black Activists based their movements largely on Malcolm X and his teachings. The Black Power movement, the Black Arts movement, and the widespread adoption of the slogan "Black is beautiful" can all trace their roots to Malcolm X.

"Freedom has never been free..."

"When you hate, the only person that suffers is you because most of the people you hate don't know it and the rest don't care."

MEDGAR EVERS

July 2, 1925 - June 12, 1963

MEDGAR EVERS, was an African American civil rights activist in Mississippi, the state's field secretary of the NAACP, and World War II veteran, having served in the United States Army. He worked to overturn segregation at the University of Mississippi, end segregation of public facilities, and to expand opportunities for African Americans, including enforcement of voting rights. His public investigations into the 1955 killing of Chicago teenager, Emmett Till, in Mississippi, and his vocal support of Clyde Kennard, made him a prominent Black leader.

"I don't know what the future may hold,
but I know who holds the future!"

RALPH ABERNATHY

March 11, 1926 - April 17, 1990

RALPH DAVID ABERNATHY, SR. was an American civil rights activist and Christian minister. As a leader of the nonviolent Civil Rights Movement, he was a close friend and mentor of Martin Luther King, Jr. He collaborated with King to create the Montgomery Improvement Association, which led to the Montgomery Bus Boycott. He also co-founded and was an executive board member of the Southern Christian Leadership Conference (SCLC). He became president of the SCLC following the assassination of King in 1968, where he led the Poor People's Campaign in Washington, DC, among other marches and demonstrations for disenfranchised Americans. He also served as an advisory committee member of the Congress on Racial Equality (CORE).

- 1969: On the eve of the Apollo 11 launch, July 15, 1969, Abernathy arrived at Cape Canaveral with several hundred members of the Poor People's Campaign to protest the spending of government space exploration when many Americans remained poor.
- Later in 1969, Abernathy took part in a labor struggle in Charleston, South Carolina, on behalf of hospital workers for the local union,

1199B, which led to a living wage increase and improved working conditions for thousands of hospital workers.

- 1971: Abernathy addressed the United Nations about world peace.
1973: Abernathy assisted in brokering a deal between the FBI and Native American protestors during the Wounded Knee incident of 1973.
- 1977: Abernathy unsuccessfully ran for the U.S. House of Representatives for the 5th district of Georgia.
- 1982: Abernathy founded the Foundation for Economic Enterprises Development, and testified before the U.S. Congress in support of extending of the Voting Rights Act.
- 1990: Abernathy died of heart disease.

DID YOU KNOW

Abernathy is entombed in Lincoln Cemetery in Atlanta, Georgia. At his behest, his tomb has the simple inscription: "I TRIED."

"Do the best you can until you know better. Then when you know better, do better."

"When you learn, teach, when you get, give."

"If someone shows you who they really are, believe them."

"I've learned that people will forget what you said, people will forget what you did, but people will never forget how you made them feel."

"While one may encounter many defeats, one must not be defeated."

MAYA ANGELOU

April 4, 1928 - May 28, 2014

MAYA ANGELOU (born Marguerite Annie Johnson) was an American poet, singer, memoirist, and civil rights activist. She published seven autobiographies, three books of essays, several books of poetry, and is credited with a list of plays, movies, and television shows spanning over 50 years. She received dozens of awards and more than 50 honorary degrees. She was active in the Civil Rights Movement and worked with Martin Luther King, Jr. and Malcolm X. She was respected as a spokesperson for Black people and women, and her works have been considered a defense of Black culture. Her books center on themes such as racism, identity, family, and travel.

1968: Maya Angelou, despite having almost no experience, wrote, produced, and narrated *Blacks, Blues, Black!*, a ten-part series of documentaries about the connection between blues music and Black Americans' African heritage.

- 1969: Angelou wrote and published her first autobiography, *I Know Why the Caged Bird Sings*, which brought her international recognition and acclaim.
- 1971: Angelou, a prolific writer of poetry, wrote a book of poetry, a volume *Just Give Me a Cool Drink of Water 'fore I Diiie.*

- 1972: Angelou wrote a screenplay, *Georgia, Georgia*; which was the first original script by a black woman to be produced.
- 1993: Angelou recited her poem "On the Pulse of Morning" at the first inauguration of Bill Clinton.
- 1996: Angelou achieved her goal of directing a feature film, namely, *Down in the Delta*.

DID YOU KNOW

In 1951, Angelou married Tosh Angelos, a Greek electrician, former sailor, and aspiring musician. After Angelou's marriage ended in 1954, she danced professionally in clubs around San Francisco, including the nightclub the Purple Onion, where she sang and danced to calypso music. Up to that point she went by the name of "Marguerite Johnson," or "Rita," but at the strong suggestion of her managers and supporters at the Purple Onion, she changed her professional name to "Maya Angelou." It was a "distinctive name" that set her apart and captured the feel of her calypso dance performances.

“Injustice anywhere is a threat to justice everywhere…”

“Our lives begin to end the day we become silent about things that matter…”

“The ultimate measure of a man is not where he stands in moments of comfort and convenience, but where he stands at times of challenge and controversy.”

DR. MARTIN LUTHER KING, JR.

January 15, 1929 - April 4, 1968

THE REVEREND MARTIN LUTHER KING, JR. was an American Baptist minister and activist who became the most visible spokesperson and leader in the civil rights movement from 1954 until his death in 1968. Born in Atlanta, King is best known for advancing civil rights through nonviolence and civil disobedience, tactics his Christian beliefs and the nonviolent activism of Mahatma Gandhi helped inspire. Martin Luther King, Jr., stood for faith, equality, and nonviolence throughout his life.

1955: King led the 1955 Montgomery bus boycott;

1957: King became the first president of the Southern Christian Leadership Conference (SCLC);

1963: King helped organize the nonviolent protests in Birmingham, Alabama;

He also helped organize the March on Washington, where he delivered his famous "I Have a Dream" speech;

1964: King won the Nobel Peace Prize for combating racial inequality through nonviolent resistance;

1965: He helped organize the Selma to Montgomery marches;

1966: King and the SCLC took the movement north to Chicago to work on segregated housing;

1968: King was planning a national occupation of Washington, DC, to be called the Poor People's Campaign, when he was assassinated on April 4 in Memphis, Tennessee.

DID YOU KNOW

Martin Luther King, Jr's. birth name was Michael King, Jr. He was named after his father, Michael King, Sr., who was a pastor. It was after King, Sr. took a trip to Germany and was inspired by the stories of the sixteenth-century priest, Martin Luther, who had broken with the Catholic Church and started the Protestant Reformation. Then King, Sr. returned to the States, and had his name and his five-year old son's name changed to Martin Luther King, as a tribute.

"Do not call for black power or green power. Call for brain power."

"If the society today allows wrongs to go unchallenged, the impression is created that those wrongs have the approval of the majority."

"But this is the great danger America faces. That we will cease to be one nation and become instead a collection of interest groups: city against suburb, region against region, individual against individual. Each seeking to satisfy private wants."

"One thing is clear to me: we, as human beings, must be willing to accept people who are different from ourselves."

BARBARA JORDAN

February 21, 1936 - January 17, 1996

BARBARA CHARLINE JORDAN was an American lawyer, educator, and politician who was a leader of the Civil Rights Movement. A Democrat, she was the first African American elected to the Texas Senate after Reconstruction, the first Southern African American woman elected to the United States House of Representatives. She was best known for her eloquent opening statement at the House Judiciary Committee hearings during the impeachment process against Richard Nixon; and as the first African American as well as the first woman to deliver a keynote address at a Democratic National Convention.

- 1956: Barbara Jordan graduated magna cum laude from Texas Southern University, an historically-black institution.
- 1959: Jordan attended and graduated from Boston University School of Law. She taught political science at Tuskegee Institute in Alabama, for one year.
- 1960: She returned to Houston, and started a private law practice. 1962: Jordan campaigned, unsuccessfully, for the Texas House of
- Representatives, both in 1962 and 1964.

- 1966: Jordan won a seat in the Texas Senate, becoming the first African American state senator since 1883.
- 1968: Jordan was re-elected to a full term in the Texas Senate; and she served until 1972.
- 1972: Jordan was elected to the U.S. House of Representatives. 1994: President Clinton awarded her the Presidential Medal of Freedom.

DID YOU KNOW

Jordan credited a speech she heard in her high school years by Edith S. Sampson with inspiring her to become an attorney. Because of segregation, she could not attend The University of Texas at Austin and instead chose Texas Southern University, an historically-black institution, majoring in political science and history. At Texas Southern University, Jordan was a national champion debater, defeating opponents from Yale and Brown and tying Harvard University.

"When people tell me nothing has changed, I say come walk in my shoes and I will show you change."

"Our struggle is a struggle to redeem the soul of America. It's not a struggle that lasts for a few days, a few weeks, a few months, a few years. It is the struggle of a lifetime, more than one lifetime."

"Get in good trouble, necessary trouble and help redeem the soul of America."

JOHN LEWIS

February 21, 1940 - July 17, 2020

JOHN ROBERT LEWIS was an African American civil rights activist. He was born in an era of racial segregation, particularly during the Jim Crow era, He was one of the "Big Six" leaders of the civil rights movement in the 1960s. He shared this title with: Whitney Young, Jr., A. Philip Randolph, Martin Luther King, Jr., James Farmer, and Roy Wilkins. He was elected to Congress in 1986. He fought for people's rights since joining Congress in 1987. Moreover, he was a beacon in the civil rights movement, who died affectionately known as "The Conscious of the Congress."

Here are some character strengths that speak to the sacrifice, dedication and commitment John Lewis had for the Civil Rights Movement:

- 1954: John Lewis, at the age of 14, was met with disappointment after learning that the Supreme Court ruling in the 1954 landmark case Brown v. Board of Education of Topeka, in which the justices ruled unanimously that racial segregation of children in public schools was unconstitutional—didn't affect his school life.
- 1955: At the age of 15, and inspired by the sermons of Dr. Martin Luther King, Jr., John Lewis began his fight for people's rights, and

identifying ways in which he could implement the changes he wanted to see.

- 1957: At the age of 17, John Lewis attended the American Baptist Theological Seminary in Nashville, Tennessee ("ABTS"). It was at the ABTS, where John Lewis learned about nonviolent protest and helped to organize sit-ins at segregated lunch counters.
- 1961: At the age of 21, John Lewis, staunchly dedicated to the civil rights movement, began participating in the Freedom Rides of 1961. John Lewis, and the Freedom Riders, engaged in the dangerous work of challenging the segregated facilities they encountered at interstate bus terminals in the South—segregated facilities which were deemed illegal by the Supreme Court, years earlier.
- These courageous acts resulted in arrests and beatings for many of the Freedom Riders, including John Lewis.
- 1963: At the age of 23, John Lewis, became chairman of the Student Nonviolent Coordinating Committee ("SNCC"). He helped to plan the March on Washington, which occurred on 08/28/1963.
- John Lewis was the youngest speaker at the event, and gave a powerful speech that declared: "We all recognize the fact that if any radical social, political and economic changes are to take place in our society, the people, the masses, must bring them about."
- 1964: John Lewis was 24 years old when the Civil Rights Act of 1964, which forbade discrimination in voting on the basis of race, became law.
- 1965: John Lewis was 25 years old when he, Hosea Williams and Dr. Martin Luther King, Jr. set out, on March 7, 1965, and led a group of approximately 600 peaceful protestors, with the goal of marching from Selma to the state capitol of Montgomery.
- It was after crossing the Edmund Pettus Bridge, when the marchers, including John Lewis, were attacked by state troopers. John Lewis suffered a fractured skull.
- 1966: John Lewis, at the age of 26, left the Student Nonviolent Coordinating Committee.

- 1968: At the age of 28, John Lewis, devastated by the assassinations of Dr. Martin Luther King, Jr., and that of Robert Kennedy, continue his work to enfranchise minorities.
- 1970: At the age of 30, John Lewis became director of the Voter Education Project; and during his tenure, he helped to register millions of minority voters.
- 1980: At the age of 41, John Lewis ran for political office; and won a seat on the Atlanta City Council.
- 1986: At the age of 46, John Lewis was elected to the House of Representatives. For the next 30 years, while in office, John Lewis consistently called for improvements in education, healthcare reform, and measures to fight poverty.
- 2016: After the mass shooting which took place on June 12, 2016, in Orlando Florida, on June 22, 2016, John Lewis, at the age of 76, organized and led at sit-in on the floor of the House of Representatives – having garnered the support of approximately 40 House Democrats. The goal was to bring attention and force Congress to address gun violence by taking definitive legislative action. He stated:
- "We have been too quiet for too long…There comes a time when you have to say something. You have to make a little noise. You have to move your feet. This is the time!"
- 2020: At the age of 80, on July 17, 2020, John Lewis passed away.

DID YOU KNOW

After former President Barack Obama won the presidency in 2008, Lewis (at the age of 68), stated that "When we were organizing voter-registration drives, going on the Freedom Rides, sitting in, coming here to Washington for the first time, getting arrested, going to jail, being beaten, I never thought—I never dreamed—of the possibility that an African American would one day be elected president of the United States."

In 2008, "At the luncheon following the swearing in ceremony [of President Barack Obama], John Lewis approached President Obama with a commemorative photograph and asked him [President Obama] to sign it.

The President wrote, “Because of you, John. Barack Obama.” [citing from an article written by David Remnick, an editor with The New Yorker]. Remnick, David. “The President’s Hero”. *The New Yorker.* January 26, 2009.

On February 15, 2011, at the age of 71, John Lewis was presented with the 2010 Medal of Freedom—the highest honor awarded to civilians. President Barack Obama had the honor of presenting this medal to John Lewis.

"Yes we can!"

"Now, as a nation, we don't promise equal outcomes, but we were founded on the idea everybody should have an equal opportunity to succeed. No matter who you are, what you look like, where you come from, you can make it. That's an essential promise of America. Where you start should not determine where you end up."

"My fellow Americans, we are and always will be a nation of immigrants. We were strangers once, too."

BARACK OBAMA

August 5, 1961 - Present

BARACK HUSSEIN OBAMA, III, is an American politician and attorney who served as the 44th President of the United States from 2009 to 2017. A member of the Democratic Party, he was the first African American president of the United States. He previously served as a U.S. Senator from Illinois from 2005 to 2008, and an Illinois State Senator from 1997 to 2004. Barack Obama has accomplished things that most people can only dream of. He was the first African American to assume the presidency and served for two terms; and Obama is a bestselling author and philanthropist.

CITATIONS

IDA B. WELLS:

By Cihak and Zima - https://www.nytimes.com/2020/08/12/arts/19th-amendment-blackwomens-suffrage-photos.html, Public Domain, https://commons.wikimedia.org/w/index.php?curid=93448526.

MARY CHURCH TERRELL:

[Mary Church Terrell, three-quarter length portrait, seated, facing front] Library of Congress Prints and Photographs Division Washington, DC. 20540 USA http://hdl.loc.gov/loc.pnp/pp.print.

W.E.B. DU BOIS:

W.E.B. (William Edward Burghardt) Du Bois, 1868-1963 Library of Congress Prints and Photographs Division Washington, DC. 20540 USA http://hdl.loc.gov/loc.pnp/pp.print.

JAMES WELDON JOHNSON:

[James Weldon Johnson, half-length portrait at desk with telephone]

- Digital ID: (b&w film copy neg.) cph 3a43308 http://hdl.loc.gov/loc.pnp/cph.3a43308.
- Reproduction Number: LC-USZ62-42992 (b&w film copy neg.).

MARY MCLEOD BETHUNE:

By Carl Van Vechten - This image is available from the United States Library of Congress's

Prints and Photographs division under the digital ID van.5a51728; Public Domain, https://commons.wikimedia.org/w/index.php?curid=2766651.

THURGOOD MARSHALL:

Library of Congress Prints and Photographs Division, U.S. News & World Report Magazine

Photograph Collection. LC-DIG-ppmsc-01271 O'Halloran, Thomas J., photographer, Date created: 1957 Sep. 17.

ADAM CLAYTON POWELL:

James J. Kriegman, Public domain, via Wikimedia Commons https://upload.wikimedia.org/wikipedia/commons/b/bc/Adam_Clayon_Powell_Jr.jpg.

ROSA PARKS:

By Unknown author - USIA / National Archives and Records Administration Records of the U.S.

Information Agency Record Group 306, Public Domain, https://commons.wikimedia.org/w/index.php?curid=4344206.

JAMES FARMER:

Trikosko, Marion S, photographer. *James Farmer at a meeting of American Society of Newspaper Editors, bust portrait, seated at a table before a microphone / MST.* , 1964. Photograph. https://www.loc.gov/item/2003688125/.

SHIRLEY CHISHOLM:

O'Halloran, Thomas J, photographer. *Congresswoman Shirley Chisholm announcing hercandidacy for presidential nomination / TOH.* Washington D.C, 1972. Photograph.

https://www.loc.gov/item/2003688123/.

MALCOLM X:

Malcolm X, Martin Luther King press conference, March 26, 1964
Public Domain photo by Marion S. Trikosko, Courtesy Library of Congress (2003688131).

MEDGAR EVERS:

Medgar Evers, head-and-shoulders portrait, facing right, wearing jacket and tie., 1963.
Photograph. https://www.loc.gov/item/93516441/.

RALPH ABERNATHY:

Leffler, Warren K, photographer. *Reverend Ralph David Abernathy, head-and-shoulders portrait, facing right, speaking at a National Press Club luncheon, Washington, DC. / WKL.* , 1968. [14 June] Photograph. https://www.loc.gov/item/2018664078/.

DR. MARTIN LUTHER KING, JR.:

Wikimedia Commons contributors, "File:Martin Luther King, Jr..jpg," *Wikimedia Commons, the free media repository,*https://commons.wikimedia.org/w/index.php?title=File:Martin_Luther_King,_Jr..jpg&oldid=638442244 (accessed May 8, 2022).

BARBARA JORDAN:

"No Known Restrictions: Barbara Jordan Speaking at the Democratic National Convention by Warren K. Leffler, July 1976 (LOC)" by pingnews.com is marked with CC PDM 1.0.

MAYA ANGELOU:

Wikimedia Commons contributors, "File: Angelou at Clinton inauguration (cropped 2).jpg," *Wikimedia Commons, the free media repository,* https://commons.wikimedia.org/w/index.php?title=File:Angelou_at_Clinton_inauguration_(cropped_2).jpg&oldid=646833321 (accessed May 8, 2022).

JOHN LEWIS:

Retrieved from "https://commons.wikimedia.org/w/index.php?title=File:John_Lewis-2006_(cropped).jpg&oldid=623995151."

BARACK OBAMA:

Wikimedia Commons contributors, "File: Official portrait of Barack Obama.jpg," *Wikimedia Commons, the free media repository,*https://commonswikimedia.org/w/index.php?title=File:Official_portrait_of_Barack_Obama.jpg&oldid=611615614 (accessed May 8, 2022).

FANNE LOU HAMER:

Leffler, Warren K, photographer. *Fannie Lou Hamer, Mississippi Freedom Democratic Party delegate, at the Democratic National Convention, Atlantic City, New Jersey, August/ WKL.* New Jersey Atlantic City, 1964. Photograph. https://www.loc.gov/item/2003688126/.

MARCUS GARVEY:

Marcus Garvey, -1940. , 1924. Aug. 5. Photograph. https://www.loc.gov/item/2003653533/.

NANNIE HELEN BURROUGHS:

Nannie Helen Burroughs. , None. [Between 1900 and 1920] Photograph. https://www.loc.gov/item/2002708615/.

ABOUT THE AUTHOR

As an African American mother, wife, and advocate for social change, Deidra, by using her voice, identity, purpose, and lived experiences, finds herself on a mission to educate as many of our youth as possible about the value of investing in themselves and learning about their history.

Deidra reminds our youth, especially our Black and brown children, that our ancestors worked hard and brilliantly at paving the way so that we could work hard and diligently to pay it forward. She does not let us forget about the men and women who fought for our rights and liberties as they sacrificed their lives so that we could be free—free physically, free mentally, and free emotionally.

In 1996, as a single mom and after nine years of full-time employment with TIAA-CREF, a Manhattan-based company, Deidra quit her job as a commercial real estate paralegal to attend law school. In 1999, after graduating City University of New York School of Law, Deidra worked as a public defender with The Legal Aid Society in Bronx County. In 2004, nearly five years later, Deidra left The Legal Aid Society to establish her own firm, the Law Offices of Deidra R. Moore, P.C. Deidra advises and litigates on all aspects of matrimonial law, guardianship matters, trusts and estates law, elder law, and wrongful death cases.

After twenty years of being a practicing attorney, Deidra's career pivoted to becoming a published author. In 2022 she authored her first book, *From Me to You: The Power of Storytelling and Its Inherent Generational Wealth—An African American Story.*

"If you are not willing to learn, no one can help you.
If you are determined to learn, no one can stop you!"
-Zig Ziglar

DeidraMoore.com

DMJ-Voice, Identity and Purpose

@DeidraMoore2253

@DMoore2253

@Deidra Moore-Janvier

You are Beautiful.

You are Loved.

You have Civil Rights.

Your life does matter.

Racism is not your burden to carry.

YOU ARE NOT THE ROOT CAUSE OF OTHER PEOPLE'S IGNORANCE, INSECURITIES, AND STEREOTYPES.

There are more good people in the world than there are bad.

You have complete control over only one thing in the universe: your thinking!

"ONE OF THE LESSONS THAT I GREW UP WITH WAS TO ALWAYS STAY TRUE TO YOURSELF AND NEVER LET WHAT SOMEBODY ELSE SAYS DISTRACT YOU FROM YOUR GOALS."

- MICHELLE OBAMA

"Knowing is Not Enough; We Must Apply. Wishing is Not Enough; We Must Do."

- Johann Wolfgang Von Goethe

Always remember: Make your life a masterpiece; imagine no limitations on what you can be, have, or do.

"The way to get started is to quit talking and begin doing." - Walt Disney